Carlos Marcello, Petitioner, v. Robert F. Kennedy, Attorney General of the United States, et al. U.S. Supreme Court Transcript of Record with Supporting Pleadings

JACK WASSERMAN, L PAUL WININGS

Carlos Marcello, Petitioner, v. Robert F. Kennedy, Attorney General of the United States, et al.
Petition / JACK WASSERMAN / 1962 / 931 / 373 U.S. 933 / 83 S.Ct. 1536 / 10 L.Ed.2d 692 / 3-14-1963
Carlos Marcello, Petitioner, v. Robert F. Kennedy, Attorney General of the United States, et al.
Brief in Opposition (P) / L PAUL WININGS / 1962 / 931 / 373 U.S. 933 / 83 S.Ct. 1536 / 10 L.Ed.2d 692 / 5-13-1963

Carlos Marcello, Petitioner, v. Robert F.
Kennedy, Attorney General of the United
States, et al. U.S. Supreme Court Transcript of
Record with Supporting Pleadings

Table of Contents

SUPREME COURT OF THE UNITED STATES

OCTOBER TERM, 1962

No. 931

CARLOS MARCELLO,

Petitioner,

v.

ROBERT F. KENNEDY, Attorney General of the United States and RAYMOND F. FARRELL, Commissioner of the Immigration and Naturalization Service,

Respondents.

PETITION FOR A WRIT OF CERTIORARI TO THE UNITED STATES COURT OF APPEALS FOR THE DISTRICT OF COLUMBIA CIRCUIT.

Jack Wasserman,
David Carliner,
    Warner Building,
    Washington 4, D. C.,
Attorneys for Petitioner.

INDEX

CITATIONS

Cases:

—6232-3

SUPREME COURT OF THE UNITED STATES

OCTOBER TERM, 1962

No.

CARLOS MARCELLO,

Petitioner,

v.

ROBERT F. KENNEDY, ATTORNEY GENERAL OF THE UNITED STATES AND RAYMOND F. FARRELL, COMMISSIONER OF THE IMMIGRATION AND NATURALIZATION SERVICE,

Respondents.

PETITION FOR A WRIT OF CERTIORARI TO THE UNITED STATES COURT OF APPEALS FOR THE DISTRICT OF COLUMBIA CIRCUIT.

Petitioner prays that a writ of certiorari issue to review the judgment of the United States Court of Appeals for the District of Columbia Circuit vacating a judgment of the District Court and remanding the cause with directions to dismiss the complaint.

Opinions Below

The opinion of the Court of Appeals has not yet been reported and is set forth in the Appendix at pp. 15-21. The opinions of the District Court are reported at 194 F. Supp. 748, 750, and are set forth in the Appendix at pp. 23-32.

Jurisdiction

The judgment of the Court of Appeals was entered on December 20, 1962. Jurisdiction of this Court is invoked under 28 U.S.C. 1254(1).

Questions Presented

1. Where a three judge District Court is convened to consider a request for injunctive relief and a claim of unconstitutionality of a federal statute, is it authorized to remand the cause to a single judge to consider a motion for summary judgment?

2. Where, after deportation to Guatemala, an alien asserts a justiciable controversy in his complaint as to the propriety of such deportation does such issue become moot by his return to the United States requiring the District Court as a matter of discretion to dismiss a declaratory judgment action and vacate a judgment filed previous to his return here?

3. Where it has been determined in administrative deportation proceedings (5 I & N Dec. 261) and subsequent judicial proceedings, *Marcello v. Bonds*, 349 U.S. 302 (1955), that an alien was born in Tunis, Africa, is it proper for the Immigration Service to represent to Guatemala that he was born in Guatemala and arrange for his deportation to that country upon a claim of Guatemalan citizenship based upon a forged Guatemalan birth record?

4. Where deportation to Guatemala has been accomplished by false representations of our Immigration Service that an alien is a native and citizen of Guatemala, contrary to administrative and judicial decisions as to his place of birth, where under Guatemalan law he is an inadmissible alien, where acceptance by Guatemala was based upon the aforesaid false representations, and where Guatemala

subsequently repudiated such acceptance and deported the alien for illegal entry, was Guatemala willing to accept the alien and was deportation there lawful and proper?

5. Where in administrative and judicial proceedings Tunis, Africa, had been determined to be an alien's place of birth, was it proper for the Immigration Service to advise him at 1:00 p.m., on April 4, 1961, that he was born in Guatemala, was a citizen thereof, and remove him from the United States at 1:35 p.m., that day bound for Guatemala without affording him an opportunity to contest the legality of such new administrative determination?

6. Where an attorney accompanying the said alien on April 4, 1961, was detained by the Immigration Service during the period that the aforesaid alien was being driven to the airport for deportation, was the alien deprived of the effective assistance of counsel vitiating his deportation?

Constitutional Provisions, Statutes and Regulations Involved

The Fifth Amendment provides in part that no person shall:

"be deprived of life, liberty, or property, without due process of law."

The Eighth Amendment provides:

"Excessive bail shall not be required, nor excessive fines imposed, nor cruel and unusual punishment inflicted."

Section 243(a) of the Immigration and Nationality Act of 1952, 8 U.S.C. 1253(a) provides:

"The deportation of an alien in the United States provided for in this Act, or any other Act or treaty, shall be directed by the Attorney General to a country promptly designated by the alien if that country is willing to accept him into its territory. * * * [Where such designation is unavailable] deportation of such alien shall be directed to any country of which such alien is a subject, national, or citizen if such country is willing to accept him into its territory. If the Government of such country fails to finally advise the Attorney General or the alien * * * whether that government will or will not accept such alien into its territory, then such deportation shall be directed by the Attorney General within his discretion and without necessarily giving any priority or preference because of their order as herein set forth either—

"(1) to the country from which such alien last entered the United States;

* * * * *

"(3) to the country in which he was born;

* * * * *

"(7) if deportation to any of the foregoing places or countries is impracticable, inadvisable, or impossible, then to any country which is willing to accept such alien into its territory."

8 Code of Federal Regulations 243.1 provides:

"Issuance of warrants of deportation; country to which alien shall be deported; cost of detention; care and attention of alien—(a) Issuance. A warrant of deportation shall be based upon the final order of deportation and shall be issued by a district director or an immigration officer acting for him."

Statement

This action for declaratory judgment and injunctive relief seeks to review an executed order of deportation claimed to be illegal and in violation of petitioner's constitutional rights.

Petitioner asserts in his complaint that he is a native of Tunis, Africa (R. 4, par. 2), and that he came to the United States in 1910 at the age of eight months, that he was here until April 4, 1961, when he was forcibly removed to Guatemala by respondents pursuant to an order of deportation for a 1938 violation of the Marihuana Tax Act. He alleges that although it had been decided judicially *(Marcello v. Bonds,* 349 U.S. 302) and administratively (5 I & N Dec. 261) that he was born in Tunis, Africa, upon the basis of a false birth record showing birth in Guatemala, his removal to that country was illegally effectuated (R. 5, 6, par. 10-20). Respondents admit that a Guatemalan birth certificate was utilized to secure removal of petitioner to Guatemala. (Affidavit of E. DeWitt Marshall of April 10, 1961, R. 18, 19; Guatemalan Reentry Permit of March 15, 1961, R. 63). Respondents, precluded by *Marcello v. Bonds,* 349 U.S. 302 (1955), do not now claim that petitioner was born in Guatemala. See Item No. 1 of petitioner's statement under Rule 9, admitted by respondents (R. 29, 48). The complaint asserts that respondents arranged petitioner's acceptance as a deportee by Guatemala upon false representations as to his place of birth, that petitioner was in fact inadmissible to Guatemala, and that had the true facts been revealed Guatemala would not have accepted him as a deportee. Guatemala subsequently repudiated such acceptance and deported Marcello for illegal entry (R. 53). It is asserted that his removal to Guatemala by false representations was illegal (R. 6, par. 16-20).

On September 16, 1955, Justice Black ordered that petitioner be given three days' notice prior to any proposed deportation. Thereafter, a stipulation of the Solicitor General and counsel was substituted for this order. Notwithstanding, petitioner was seized when he reported to the Immigration Service at 1.00 p.m. on April 4, 1961, and deported at 1.35 p.m. that same day without any notice or opportunity to secure clothes, funds or communicate with his family or immigration attorneys. An attorney who accompanied petitioner was unlawfully detained in respondents' automobile thereby depriving petitioner of the effective assistance of counsel (R. 6-8, par. 22-30). Affidavits of respondents admit the summary manner in which petitioner was seized and removed without advance notice (R. 14, 21).

Petitioner asserts that he was never in Guatemala previously, is unfamiliar with its customs and language, and asserts that the statute authorizing his deportation there as construed and applied to him is unconstitutional in that it violates due process and the prohibition against cruel and unusual punishment (R. 8, par. 31-33).

Request was made to declare petitioner's deportation to Guatemala illegal, to enjoin enforcement of the deportation statute and to require respondents to authorize petitioner's return here.

Respondents filed no answer to petitioner's complaint, but moved to dismiss alleging *inter alia* (R. 11) that the court lacked jurisdiction and that the complaint failed to state a cause of action. Opposing affidavits were filed by both parties (R. 9-24, 31-42, 51-55).

Proceedings Below

(i) *The Three Judge Court.* At petitioner's request and upon the basis of *Wolf* v. *Boyd*, 287 F.2d 520 (C.A. 9, 1961), a three judge District Court was convened. The third cause of action herein attacked removal to Guatemala as contrary to the Fifth and Eighth Amendments and injunctive relief was requested. The three judge court dissolved itself and remitted the cause to District Judge Holtzoff on May 12, 1961, for further proceedings after entry of an order which recited (R. 28):

> "The court having concluded that no injunction shall issue and being satisfied that the allegations of plaintiff's complaint present only a claim of unconstitutionality of the result obtained by the use of a statute which has not been attacked as unconstitutional * * *."

(ii) *The District Court.* Judge Holtzoff treated respondents' motion to dismiss (R. 11) as a motion for summary judgment. The matter came on before him on cross motions for summary judgment (R. 29).

Despite the requirement of the statute that deportation first be to the country of an alien's citizenship and thereafter only to another country willing to accept him *where deportation elsewhere is impracticable* [8 U.S.C. 1253(a)], despite the Government's acknowledgment that deportation to Guatemala was to Marcello's asserted country of citizenship (R. 16, 43), a fact verified by the reentry permit (R. 63), despite the misrepresentations perpetrated upon the Government of Guatemala, the District Court upheld deportation there pursuant to 8 U.S.C. 1253(a)(7) (R. 59, 61).

Judge Holtzoff found that Guatemala accepted Marcello as a deportee even though that Government erroneously received him as a Guatemalan citizen upon false representations by American officials and later repudiated this acceptance (R. 61). He found that no rights of petitioner had been violated, although he questioned the manner in which deportation was accomplished (Transcript, May 19, 1961, p. 17). Judgment was entered for respondents (R. 49) and motions for reconsideration (R. 50) and to vacate (R. 57) were denied.

(iii) *The Court of Appeals,* by a divided vote, vacated the judgment of Judge Holtzoff holding that petitioner's return to the United States subsequent to the District Court's ruling rendered the issue of reentry moot and required dismissal of the declaratory judgment complaint as a matter of discretion (Appendix, pp. 16-18). This view was adopted by the Court of Appeals despite agreement by both parties that no mootness surrounded the issue herein as to the legality of the petitioner's deportation. On the contrary, such issue is now pending in several subsequent proceedings noted by the Court below (Appendix, pp. 17, 18).

Reasons for Granting the Writ

1. The decision below is contrary to *Schneider* v. *Rusk* (No. 251, October Term, 1962); *Query* v. *United States,* 316 U.S. 486 (1941); and *Wolf* v. *Boyd,* 287 F.2d 520 (C.A. 9, 1961). Issues of recurring significance in practice and procedure before three judge courts are involved, as well as the constitutionality of a deportation statute authorizing removal of an alien to any country willing to receive him. 8 U.S.C. 1253(a)(7).

Petitioner, a native of Tunis [*Marcello* v. *Bonds,* 349 U.S. 302 (1954)], alleged in his complaint, *inter alia,* that:

"As construed and applied to plaintiff, the Immigration and Nationality Act authorizing his deportation.

to a country where he never lived and with whose
customs and language he is unfamiliar, violated due
process of law and the constitutional prohibition
against the imposition of cruel and unusual
punishment.''

(Par. 33 of Complaint, R. 8.)

A three judge District Court was convened and it upheld
the constitutionality of the statute [8 U.S.C. 1253(a)(7)]
authorizing deportation to any country willing to receive
an alien into its territory. It then remanded the cause to
a single judge with an opinion stating, 194 F. Supp. 748,
749 (R. 27):

"At most the allegations of plaintiff's complaint
present a claim of unconstitutionality of the result
obtained by the use of a statute which is not attacked
as unconstitutional. The latter petition does not
require a three judge court.''

The complaint herein is worded exactly the same as that
in *Mascitti* v. *McGrath,* Civil Action No. 5148-50 (D.C.
Dist. of Col.), in which case a direct appeal was granted
to this Court. The cause was consolidated and decided
under the title of *Harisiades* v. *Shaughnessy,* 342 U.S.
580 (1952). Our complaint is likewise similar to that
presented in *Schneider* v. *Rusk, supra.*

The basis for the language in Paragraph 33 of our complaint is *Query* v. *United States,* 316 U.S. 486 (1941),
where it was said:

"Here a substantial charge has been made that a
state statute as applied to the complainants violates
the Constitution. Under such circumstances, we have
held that relief in the form of an injunction can be
afforded only by a three judge court * * *.''

Here, the complaint attacked the constitutionality of 8 U.S.C. 1253(a)(7) authorizing deportation of petitioner to any country willing to accept him. Injunctive relief was requested. The three judge court denied such relief, passing upon the constitutionality of the statute. As noted by Judge Holtzoff (R. 62):

> "The three judge court was convened, *upheld the constitutionality of the statute,* denied a motion for a preliminary injunction, dissolved the three judge court, and remitted the remainder of the issues to me as a single judge for disposition." 194 F. Supp. 753.

If the complaint herein did not attack the constitutionality of the statute, the three judge court erroneously passed upon the said issue. Nevertheless, Judge Holtzoff interpreted the complaint, as we intended it, as an attack on the constitutionality of the statute. The Court of Appeals gave a similar construction to the complaint (R. 230).

Wolf v. *Boyd*, 287 F. 2d 520 (C.A. 9, 1961), holds that the constitutional attack herein is of a substantial nature. Judge Holtzoff so held herein when he requested the convocation of a three judge court over the objections of respondents. The three judge court should have passed upon the motion for summary judgment. The ruling below remanding the motion to a single judge was contrary to *Schneider* v. *Rusk, supra,* and *Wolf* v. *Boyd, supra.*

2. The decision below involves an important issue of federal practice relating to justiciability of controversies and the availability of declaratory judgments. Over objections of both parties declaratory judgment has been foreclosed to petitioner upon the ground of alleged mootness and the subsequent appearance of forums to litigate the issues herein. We submit the Court of Appeals erroneously

found abuse of discretion in the District Court's assumption of jurisdiction herein.

As the Court of Appeals acknowledged (R. 231), petitioner seeks a declaration of his rights, i.e., that his deportation to Guatemala was illegal and that it was pursuant to an unconstitutional statute. Admittedly, this issue was not rendered moot by petitioner's return to the United States subsequent to the District Court's decision. Nevertheless, upon the assumption that petitioner's return here rendered moot that part of the complaint requesting reentry, the Court of Appeals proceeded to find an abuse of discretion by the District Court in retaining jurisdiction of the action.

A moot case has been defined as "one which seeks to get a judgment on a pretended controversy, when in reality there is none, or a decision in advance about a right before it has been actually asserted or contested, or a judgment upon some matter which, when rendered for any reason cannot have any practical legal effect upon a then existing controversy." *Ex parte Steele,* 162 Fed. 694, 701 (N.D. Ala., 1908); *Burrell* v. *Martin,* 232 F. 2d 33, 37 (C.A., D.C., 1955).

Here a real and ripe controversy remained over the legality of deportation to Guatemala even after petitioner's return here. If such deportation were legal, petitioner reentered illegally and became subject to criminal and new deportation penalties. 8 U.S.C. 1326, 1182(a)(17), 1251(a)(1). If such deportation were illegal, then as observed by Judge Holtzoff, his reentry would be proper (R. 60).

In the light of the actuality of this controversy, existing at the time of the District Court's judgment and continuing to the present time, discretion was appropriately exercised to review the litigation herein. *Aetna Life Ins. Co.* v. *Haworth*, 300 U.S. 227 (1936); *Perkins* v. *Elg*, 307 U.S. 325 (1938); *Meredith* v. *Winter Haven*, 320 U.S. 228, 234-236 (1943). We agree with the opinion below that the case should not have been decided in favor of respondents upon affidavits. However, we submit that petitioner's complaint should not be dismissed for lack of a ripe or real controversy.

3. This case presents an important issue in the administration of justice and in the enforcement of our immigration laws. The documentary evidence produced below (R. 18, 19, 63, 64), discloses that petitioner's deportation to Guatemala was arranged by false representations made to Guatemala by our immigration officials as to petitioner's place of birth, citizenship, occupation, and whereabouts on March 15, 1961. In the light of the high standard of conduct required by responsible governmental officials, *Berger* v. *United States*, 295 U.S. 78, 88 (1935); *United States* v. *Zborowski*, 271 F. 2d 661 (C.A. 2, 1959); *United States* v. *Universita*, 298 F. 2d 365 (C.A. 2, 1962), in view of the necessity of supplying a receiving country with full and true information about an alien, *U.S. ex rel. Scala Di Felice* v. *Shaughnessy*, 114 F. Supp. 791 (D.C. S.D.N.Y., 1953), and considering the requirement that a receiving country express its willingness to accept a deportee, *Lu.* v. *Rogers*, 164 F. Supp. 320 (D.C., Dist. of Col.), affirmed 262 F. 2d 471 (C.A., D.C., 1958)—we submit that there was no true and valid acceptance of petitioner by Guatemala rendering his deportation valid.

4. The deportation of petitioner was accomplished after summary notice to him of thirty-five minutes. Petitioner's attorney was detained by immigration authorities and was prevented from rendering him any assistance (R. 40, 36). This nullification of the right to counsel in an immigration

case presents a significant constitutional issue. *Handlovitz* v. *Adcock*, 80 F. Supp. 425 (E.D. Mich., 1948); *Powell* v. *Alabama*, 284 U.S. 45 (1931).

Conclusion

For the reasons set forth above, it is respectfully submitted that the petition for a writ of certiorari should be granted.

JACK WASSERMAN,
DAVID CARLINER,
   Warner Building,
   Washington 4, D. C.,
Attorneys for Petitioner.

APPENDIX

United States Court of Appeals for the District of
Columbia Circuit

No. 16,553

Carlos Marcello, appellant,

v.

Robert F. Kennedy, Attorney General of the United
States, et al., *Appellees.*

Appeal from the United States District Court for the
District of Columbia

Decided December 20, 1962

Before Wilbur K. Miller, Washington and Bastian,
Circuit Judges.

Washington, *Circuit Judge:* This is an immigration case.
It is a sequel to *Marcello* v. *Bonds,* 349 U.S. 302, in which
the Supreme Court declared Carlos Marcello to be a deportable alien. That was in 1955. Since that time numerous
efforts have been made by the Government to effect his deportation. Roadblocks have been placed in its path by
litigation brought by Marcello, as well as by refusals by
other countries to accept him.

Finally, on April 4, 1961, the Government physically removed Marcello from Louisiana to Guatemala. On the
following day, Marcello's attorneys brought this suit on
his behalf in the United States District Court for the District of Columbia. The complaint alleged that the Government had utilized a false birth certificate to procure his
entry into Guatemala; that the deportation was accomplished in violation of a stipulation by the Solicitor General that Marcello would receive three days notice of any
proposed deportation; that he was denied the assistance of
counsel; and that the statutory provision for deportation
to any country willing to receive an alien (8 U.S.C. § 1253
(a)(7)) is unconstitutional. The complaint asked (1) for

a declaration that appellant's deportation to Guatemala was illegal; (2) that enforcement of the statute be enjoined; and (3) that the immigration authorities be ordered to authorize his reentry into this country.

On cross-motions, the District Court granted summary judgment for the Government, and dismissed the complaint, under date of May 24, 1961. A motion by Marcello for reconsideration was denied on June 5. A motion was then made by Marcello on June 9th to vacate the summary judgment under Fed.R.Civ.P. 60(b), attaching an affidavit of counsel that Marcello had surrendered himself to the Immigration and Naturalization Service in New Orleans on June 5th. A hearing on this motion was held on June 16, 1961, at which it appeared that Marcello had reentered the United States in some fashion, and that the Government had begun a criminal prosecution against him in New Orleans. On June 20, 1961, the District Court denied the motion to vacate; on June 26, it filed an opinion purporting to decide the case on the merits, in favor of the Government. See 194 F.Supp. 750. Appeal was taken from the summary judgment and from the court's orders of June 5 and June 20.

It is to be noted, in the first place, that the Government filed no counterclaim for a declaration that Marcello was properly deported, and no declaratory judgment to that effect was actually issued. Judge Holtzoff's opinion does not purport to be a judgment: it is an explanation of his views and of his refusal to vacate the existing judgment. Accordingly, the binding effect on Marcello of the judgment below—as a decision on the merits rather than as a mere dismissal of his complaint—may well be subject to some question.[1]

In our view, the District Court should simply have dismissed the complaint, in the exercise of its informed discretion. By June 20th it was clear that the question of reentry was moot, since Marcello was back in the United States. The only possible relief asked in the complaint

---

[1] *Cf.* BORCHARD, DECLARATORY JUDGMENTS at 812 ff. (2d Ed. 1941).

which did not become moot was a declaration of rights. But such a declaration must settle a case or controversy. It should not be issued—either formally or informally—where (as here) its significance and effect remain in doubt.

By June 20 it was also clear that Marcello's defense to the pending criminal prosecution would be that his deportation to Guatemala was illegal. Further, it was clear that the Government was issuing a new deportation order against Marcello; that this order could and in all probability would be subjected to judicial review; and that the question of the legality of the deportation to Guatemala would be a vital issue on review. All these proceedings, including any judgment of conviction rendered in the criminal prosecution, would be reviewable in the Fifth Circuit Court of Appeals.[2]

In its brief the Government, in urging us to affirm the judgment below on the merits, states that "appellant's illegal reentry has produced a criminal prosecution and a new deportation proceeding which may both essentially rest upon the judgment of the District Court below. In view of its potential effect on those proceedings, the declaratory aspect of his case obviously still presents a live controversy. . . . The whole object of the declaratory judgment procedure is to remove uncertainty from legal relations, by expeditiously settling disputed issues 'on which a whole complex of rights may depend.' " This statement of the situation appears to us to demand the very opposite conclusion from that which the Government (and appellant also, it may be mentioned) suggests. We think that under these circumstances a court sitting in the District of Columbia should not have attempted to settle the questions raised by this complaint,[3] or to pass upon the merits of Marcello's position, either favorably or unfavorably, particularly on a record consisting solely of affidavits and exhibits. We assume that in the criminal prosecution Mar-

---

[2] See Act of September 26, 1961, 75 STAT. 651, 8 U.S.C. § 1105a.

[3] Cf. Williams v. Virginia Military Institute, 91 U.S.App.D.C. 206, 198 F.2d 980 (1952), cert. denied, 345 U.S. 904 (1953).

cello would assert that he was entitled to produce live witnesses and have the jury decide issues of credibility. We assume that he would likewise assert that the trial judge in the criminal case would not be bound to accept the result here reached by Judge Holtzoff, on a different record, and that the judge would not be bound to instruct the jury as a matter of law on the basis thereof that Marcello's deportation to Guatemala was legal. (We do not, of course, decide or infer that any of these assertions would be valid: we merely point out that issues of this sort would be almost certain to arise.)

It is true that Marcello initiated the action here, and there is much to be said for holding him to the result. But in a criminal case the burden of proof is on the Government, and the question whether it has met its burden should be decided in the criminal proceeding, on the record there made. We are also aware that as of May 24, 1961, the date the judgment of dismissal was entered, the circumstances on which we now rely either had not come to pass or had not been made known to the District Court. Consequently, the initial assumption of jurisdiction can hardly be said to have constituted an abuse of discretion. These facts had come to light, however, by the time appellant made his motion to vacate the judgment of dismissal as well as at the time Judge Holtzoff rendered his opinion explaining the basis of the dismissal. Consideration should have been given to these intervening circumstances. Cf. *McKay* v. *Clackamas County*, 349 U.S. 909 (1955), vacating 94 U.S. App.D.C. 108, 126, 219 F.2d 479, 497 (1954).

The courts have a broad measure of discretion to decline to issue declaratory judgments, see *Great Lakes Dredge & Dock Co.* v. *Huffman*, 319 U.S. 293, 300 (1943), and such discretion to decline should have been exercised in this case. Under the circumstances, "The judgment of dismissal below must therefore be affirmed, but solely on the ground that, in the appropriate exercise of the court's discretion, relief by way of a declaratory judgment should have been denied . . . ." *Great Lakes Dredge & Dock Co.* v. *Huffman, supra* at 301. To clarify the record, the judgment and orders on appeal will be vacated, and the case remanded to the District Court with directions to dismiss the complaint.

So ordered.

WILBUR K. MILLER, *Circuit Judge*, dissenting: Judge Holtzoff's opinion discussing the merits and directing summary judgment for the Government was marked "Filed" by the Clerk of the District Court on June 26, 1961, as the majority say. For that reason, they seem to treat this case as an appeal from a judgment entered June 26 pursuant to the opinion which was marked "Filed" as of that date. But the opinion was dated May 22, 1961, and the summary judgment it directed was actually filed May 24, 1961.

By motion filed May 31, 1961, Marcello asked the court to reconsider and to set aside the judgment. The motion was denied June 5. Then Marcello moved on June 9 to vacate the summary judgment of May 24. On June 20 Judge Holtzoff denied the motion to vacate and delivered a second opinion giving his reasons for doing so. (The two opinions are printed together in 194 F. Supp. 750, where the first is correctly dated May 22, 1961, and the date of the second is incorrectly given as June 23 instead of June 20.) All this occurred before June 26, the day when the majority assume the first opinion was delivered.

It may be concluded, I think, that the summary judgment would not have been filed if the judge had not authorized it, and there is no indication of authorization in the record except the opinion dated May 22. The difference is material because, when the District Court spoke by its judgment of May 24, Marcello had not returned to the United States, or at least there was nothing in the record suggesting he had done so,[1] and so there was nothing to indicate mootness as to the question of re-entry. Consequently the District Court was quite justified in considering the case on the merits, and in exercising its discretion to enter summary

---

[1] The first suggestion to Judge Holtzoff that Marcello had re-entered the United States was during his consideration of the motion to vacate made on June 9 and denied June 20.

judgment for the Attorney General. That is to say, the matter of Marcello's re-entry was not moot on May 22 when the opinion was delivered, nor on May 24 when the summary judgment ordered by it was filed. The majority erroneously conclude that Judge Holtzoff's summary judgment dealt with the factual situation as it was said to exist on June 20, when the motion to vacate the judgment of May 24 was denied, or on June 26 when the opinion of May 22 was marked "Filed." In fact, the judgment of May 24 dealt with the situation as it existed on that date, and the orders of June 5 and June 20 denying the motions to reconsider and vacate dealt with the propriety of the judgment of May 24.

The notice of appeal says nothing of June 26. It shows Marcello was appealing from the summary judgment of May 24, the order of June 5 denying reconsideration, and the order of June 20 denying the motion to vacate. Consequently, we must determine the propriety of the summary judgment of May 24 on the record as it then existed. So considered, I think it is clear that the summary judgment should be affirmed for the reasons given in Judge Holtzoff's original opinion of May 22. Being of that view, I think the motion for reconsideration was properly denied on June 5.

There remains only the question whether the District Court correctly denied the motion to vacate. Implicit in the majority opinion is the notion that Judge Holtzoff should have granted the motion to vacate the summary judgment of May 24 and instead should have declined jurisdiction, merely because he was told at some later date that Marcello was back in the United States. But, as I have said, the District Court had spoken as of May 24, and a subsequent development—even if established—did not change the situation with respect to which it had adjudicated the rights of the parties by granting summary judgment to the Attorney General. It can hardly be said that, because of an event which occurred in June, the District Court did not appropriately exercise its jurisdiction to decide the case on facts submitted to it in May. Surely a judgment which decides an existing case or controversy is not mooted by an event which occurs after its entry.

The majority opinion seems to me to be more favorable to Marcello than he deserves. It assumes that the summary judgment of May 24, 1961, based on the opinion of May 22, would somehow prejudice Marcello in defending himself against an anticipated criminal indictment in another jurisdiction. In the first place, I do not think the judgment in a civil action here would have any effect in such a criminal action; and, in the second place, if the May 24 judgment has such an effect, Marcello should not be heard to complain, as he instituted the action in which the judgment was entered.

I note the Attorney General opposed the motion to vacate the judgment even though it was said in June, when the motion was made and argued, that Marcello had then returned to the United States. He did not suggest that Judge Holtzoff should vacate his judgment because of a later development or because of prospective litigation in another forum. I think the motion to vacate was properly denied.

I would affirm on the basis of Judge Holtzoff's opinion of May 22.

UNITED STATES COURT OF APPEALS FOR THE DISTRICT OF
COLUMBIA CIRCUIT

No. 16,553

September Term, 1962.

CARLOS MARCELLO, *Appellant,*

v.

ROBERT F. KENNEDY, ATTORNEY GENERAL OF THE UNITED
STATES, *et al., Appellees.*

Appeal from the United States District Court for the
District of Columbia.

Before: WILBUR K. MILLER, WASHINGTON and BASTIAN,
Circuit Judges.

JUDGMENT

This cause came on to be heard on the record on appeal
from the United States District Court for the District of
Columbia, and was argued by counsel.

ON CONSIDERATION WHEREOF, it is ordered and adjudged
by this court that the judgment and orders of the District
Court on appeal herein are vacated, and that this cause is
returned to the District Court with directions to dismiss
the complaint.

Per Curiam.

Dated: December 20, 1962.

Separate dissenting opinion by Circuit Judge Wilbur
K. Miller.

UNITED STATES DISTRICT COURT FOR THE DISTRICT OF
COLUMBIA

*   *   *   *   *   *   *

[Filed June 26, 1961]

OPINION

This is an action for a declaratory judgment to adjudi-
cate that the deportation of the plaintiff Marcello, which
has taken place pursuant to the provisions of the 1952
Immigration and Nationality Act, 8 U.S.C. §1251, is
invalid. The plaintiff was deported to Guatemala and,
promptly upon his deportation, his counsel filed this
action in this Court, alleging the deportation was illegal.[1]
The matter is before the Court on cross-motions for
summary judgment.

The administrative deportation proceeding was instituted on December 30, 1952, on a charge that the plaintiff
was convicted in 1938 of a violation of the Marijuana Tax
Act. On February 20, 1953, a Special Inquiry Officer of
the Immigration and Naturalization Service issued an
order of deportation after a hearing. An appeal was taken
to the Board of Immigration Appeals and on June 1, 1956,
the order of deportation was affirmed by the Board.
Immediately thereafter a series of law suits were instituted in the United States District Court for the Eastern
District of Louisiana and in this Court to set aside the
deportation order. It is not necessary to recapitulate
the long history of this litigation. Suffice it to say that on
May 31, 1955, the Supreme Court affirmed the deportation
order in *Marcello v. Bonds*, 349 U.S. 302. This decision
ended the litigation in respect to the validity of the deportation order. Thereupon, the Immigration and Naturaliza-

---

[1] Originally the defendants filed a motion to dismiss the complaint. As
it was later supplemented by affidavits the Court treated it as a motion for
summary judgment as provided by Rule 12(b) of the Federal Rules of Civil
Procedure. The plaintiff then filed a cross-motion for summary judgment.

tion Service instituted efforts to effectuate the deportation previously ordered.

An enumeration of the countries to which the deportation of a deportable alien may be effected, is found in 8 U.S.C. §1253. The purpose of this Section was obviously to accord considerable leeway to the United States to carry out such an order. It is provided in Subsection (a) that the deportation shall be directed to a country promptly designated by the alien, if that country is willing to accept him into its territory, unless the Attorney General concludes that deportation to that country would be prejudicial to the interests of the United States. It is further provided that no alien shall be permitted to make more than one such designation. Acting under this provision, on June 29, 1955, Marcello designated France as the country to which he wished to be deported. On July 21, 1955, the Immigration and Naturalization Service received a formal refusal on the part of the Government of France to accept Marcello.

The Section further provides that if the government of the country designated by the alien refuses to accept him, then the deportation may be directed to any country of which the alien is a subject, national, or citizen, if that country is willing to accept him into its territory. Failing that, the Attorney General, in his discretion, is authorized to effect deportation to any one of a number of countries, without giving any priority or preference because of the order in which they are enumerated in the statute. Thus, the first paragraph permits deportation to the country from which the alien last entered the United States; another provision authorizes deportation to the country in which he was born. There are seven different choices, and the last and seventh option is to any country which is willing to accept the alien into its territory.

After France refused to accept the alien, our Government, attempted to deport him to Italy, but the Italian Government, on August 9, 1955, withdrew permission that it had previously granted to Marcello for admission to Italy. There are some indications in the file that Marcello caused proceedings to be brought in the courts of Italy in order to secure a cancellation of his own permission to enter Italy.

Later there came into the possession of the United States a birth certificate tending to show that the plaintiff was born in Guatemala. Accordingly representations were made by officials of the United States to appropriate officials of Guatemala requesting the Government of Guatemala to accept the plaintiff if he were to be deported there. A document was then issued by the Guatemalan Government, the effect of which was to permit the plaintiff to enter that country. On April 4, 1961, the plaintiff was taken into custody by the Immigration and Naturalization Service in New Orleans and promptly deported by airplane to Guatemala, where he was permitted to land. It is claimed in behalf of the plaintiff in this action that he was not born in Guatemala, is not a citizen of Guatemala, and that, therefore, his deportation to that country was illegal.

At the outset, Government counsel contend that this action does not lie. It was held, however, in the case of *Shaughnessy* v. *Pedreiro*. 239 U.S. 48, that the validity of a deportation under the Immigration and Nationality Act of 1952, may be reviewed judicially under the Administrative Procedure Act and that such review may be had by an action for an injunction or for a declaratory judgment. It is argued that such an action lies only if it is brought while the alien is in this country; whereas, in this instance, it was instituted after the deportation had taken place and the alien was in Guatemala. The Court considers this distinction untenable. If the deportation were in fact and in law invalid, then the plaintiff would have the right to re-enter this country. Consequently, there is a justiciable controversy; there is a legal issue to be determined. Moreover, it would not do to say that the Government may deprive a person of a judicial remedy by taking prompt action and presenting the courts with a *fait accompli*. I do not think that the courts are as powerless as that.

The scope of review of a deportation order, however, is exceedingly narrow. Moreover, in this instance, it is not the original order of deportation that is presented for review. That order has already been reviewed and its validity sustained by the Supreme Court. What is presented for consideration is the question whether deportation to Guatemala was legal and valid under the deportation order.

The Government of this country, through its proper representatives, requested permission from the Government of Guatemala for Marcello to be received by that country. Such permission was granted, as evidenced by a Guatemalan document issued by its appropriate officials. On the basis of that document representatives of this Government brought the plaintiff to Guatemala, were permitted by the officials of the Guatemalan Government to land him there and leave him in that country. It is urged in behalf of the plaintiff, however, that subsequently to his arrival in that country the Guatemalan Government cancelled its prior permission and seeks to expel the plaintiff from its territory.

Counsel for the Government present a formal communication, dated May 5, 1961, directed to the United States Attorney by Katharine W. Bracken, Director of the Office of Central American and Panamanian Affairs of the Department of State, in which it is certified that the Departmen of State has received no representations from the Government of Guatemala, either oral or in writing, which in any manner qualifies or changes its original acceptance of Carlos Marcello, also known as Calogero Minacore, also known as Calogers, into its territory as a deportee from the United States. A communication from the State Department such as this imports verity. The Court may not intrude into any negotiations between the Government of the United States and the government of a foreign country. The conduct of foreign relations is left solely to the President and his subordinates.[2]

---

[2] *United States* v. *Curtiss-Wright Corp.*, 299 U.S. 304.

Whitney v. *Robertson*, 124 U.S. 190, 194.

George E. Warren Corp. v. *United States*, 94 F.2d 597, 599, where the Court stated: ". . . matters concerning the relations between the two

It is contended that the birth certificate showing that the plaintiff was born in Guatemala is a forgery and it is urged that this assertion raises an issue of fact to be tried. The Court is of the opinion, however, that the issue of fact, if there is one, is not material. The Government of Guatemala has accepted the plaintiff, and once the acceptance was acted on and the plaintiff was brought by our Government to Guatemala and landed there, the transaction is at an end.

When this action was first brought there was an application for the convening of a three-judge court on the ground that a Constitutional question was raised, namely, that Paragraph 7 of 8 U.S.C. §1253, to which reference has been made, constituted cruel and unusual punishment, in violation of the Eighth Amendment to the Constitution. With some hesitancy, this Court granted the application for the convening of a three-judge court, being motivated particularly by the fact that the Court of Appeals for the Ninth Circuit recently held that such a question was a substantial question necessitating the convening of a three-judge court.[3] The three-judge court was convened, upheld the constitutionality of the statute, denied a motion for preliminary injunction, dissolved the three-judge court, and remitted the remainder of the issues to me as a single judge for disposition.

There is no doubt that deportation, harsh as it may be at times, is not punishment in the legal sense and, therefore, does not come within the purview of the Eighth Amendment.[4]

In the light of the foregoing discussion, the Court is of the opinion that there are no issues of fact here that are

nations and their adjustment must be left to the field of diplomacy."
Z. & F. Assets Realization Corp. v. *Hull*, 72 App.D.C. 234, 238.
Latvian State Cargo & Passenger S.S. Line v. *McGrath*, 88 U.S.App.D.C. 226, 229.

[3] *Wolf* v. *Boyd*, 287 F.2d 520.

[4] *Fong Yue Ting* v. *United States*, 149 U.S. 698, 730.
Bugajewitz v. *Adams*, 228 U.S. 585, 591.
United States v. *District Director of Immigration, etc.*, 120 F.2d 762, 764.

material and further concludes that the deportation has been in accordance with statute and is not tainted with any illegality.

Accordingly, the plaintiff's motion for a summary judgment will be denied and the defendants' motion for summary judgment granted.

Counsel will submit an appropriate order.

/s/ ALEXANDER HOLTZOFF,
United States District Judge.

May 22, 1961.

[Filed May 24, 1961]

JUDGMENT

This cause having come on for hearing upon defendant's motion to dismiss (treated as a motion for summary judgment), and upon plaintiff's motion for summary judgment; and upon consideration of the said motions, the certified administrative record of the Immigration and Naturalization Service, the State Department certified statement, the affidavits and memoranda of points and authorities in support thereof; and upon consideration of the oral arguments of counsel in open court, and it appearing to the Court that there is no genuine issue of material fact and that defendants are entitled to judgment as a matter of law,

It is by the Court this 24th day of May, 1961, ORDERED, ADJUDGED AND DECREED:

(1) That defendants' motion for summary judgment be and the same hereby is granted;

(2) That plaintiff's motion for summary judgment be and the same hereby is denied; and

(3) That plaintiff's action be and the same hereby is dismissed.

/s/ ALEXANDER HOLTZOFF,
United States District Judge.

UNITED STATES DISTRICT COURT FOR THE DISTRICT OF
COLUMBIA

*   *   *   *.   *   *   *

[Filed, May 12, 1961]

OPINION OF THREE JUDGE COURT

DANAHER, *Circuit Judge*: Plaintiff on April 5, 1961, filed in the District Court an action for declaratory judgment and for other relief naming as defendants the Attorney General and the Commissioner of Immigration. The plaintiff had been arrested and summarily deported on April 4, 1961. The plaintiff moved for a preliminary and permanent injunction to require the defendants to return the plaintiff from Guatemala and to restrain the defendants from enforcing 8 U.S.C. §1253(a)(7)(1958).

Plaintiff in his "Points and Authorities" in support of his motion for injunction, argued that a substantial constitutional question was presented, arising under the Eighth Amendment, in that the alien had lived in the United States as a lawful permanent resident for more than fifty years, and that he might not, consistently with due process and the prohibition against the imposition of cruel and unusual punishments "be deported to a country where he has never been, even momentarily, where he has no duties, no residence [and] no citizenship." Additionally, it was contended, a Fifth Amendment question was presented in that consent of the Republic of Guatemala to accept the deportee had been based upon the knowingly false misrepresentation of the defendants' agents that the plaintiff had been born in Guatemala. The Government in all other proceedings against this plaintiff had contended he was a native of Tunis.

The plaintiff previously had been held deportable, *Marcello v. Bonds*, 340 U.S. 302 (1955). The Supreme Court there described Marcello as a native of Tunis, Africa.

28 U.S.C. §2282 (1958) provides:

"An interlocutory or permanent injunction restraining the enforcement, operation or execution of any Act of Congress for repugnance to the Constitution of the United States shall not be granted by any district court or judge thereof unless the application therefor is heard and determined by a district court of three judges under section 2284 of this title."

Plaintiff's "Request for Three Judge Court," accordingly and out of an abundance of caution, was submitted by Judge Holtzoff to Chief Judge Miller who by order of April 21, 1961, convoked this three judge District Court agreeably to the provisions of 28 U.S.C. §2284 (1958).

This plaintiff already was in Guatemala at the time his application for an injunction was filed. Plaintiff's motion did not allege that 8 U.S.C. §1253(a)(7) is repugnant to the Constitution of the United States, but rather that the statute, as applied and in the light of the allegations of his complaint, had become the predicate for a course of unlawful conduct on the part of the officers charged with the enforcement of the Act.

The defendants filed an opposition to the plaintiff's motion for injunction and to his request for the convening of the three judge court, and further moved for dismissal of the complaint. The case was set down for argument on May 2, 1961, when the parties appeared by counsel and were fully heard.

The court being thus advised in the premises has concluded that no injunction shall issue. We are satisfied that the provisions of 8 U.S.C. §1253 (1958) represent a constitutional exercise of congressional power. See generally, *United States* v. *Spector*, 343 U.S. 169 (1952); *Harisiades* v. *Shaughnessy*, 342 U.S. 580 (1952). At most, the allegations of plaintiff's complaint present a claim of "unconstitutionality of the result obtained by the use of a statute which is not attacked as unconstitutional. The latter petition does not require a three-judge court." *Ex*

Parte Bransford, 310 U.S. 354, 361 (1940). Our decision is that this court as presently constituted should be dissolved. Cf. *Osage Tribe of Indians* v. *Ickes,* 45 F. Supp. 179, 187 (D.D.C. 1942).

Expressly left open are such other questions as may have been raised and which may be presented in such further proceedings as the parties may be advised to pursue. The case will be remitted to District Judge Holtzoff for appropriate action, and an order will be entered accordingly.

[Filed May 12, 1961]

ORDER

Plaintiff having filed his motion for a preliminary and permanent injunction restraining the enforcement by the defendants of 8 U.S.C. §1253(a)(7), and for the hearing and consideration thereof having requested that a three-judge court be convened; Chief Judge Miller under date of April 21, 1961, having designated the undersigned as members of the court so convened; the defendants having filed their opposition to the plaintiff's said motion and to his request for a three-judge court; the case having been set for argument on May 2, 1961, when the parties appeared by counsel and were fully heard; and the court having concluded that no injunction shall issue and being satisfied that the allegations of plaintiff's complaint present only a claim of unconstitutionality of the result obtained by the use of a statute which has not been attacked as unconstitutional; and the court having decided that, the premises considered, a three-judge court is not required, all in accordance with an opinion of the court this day filed; now in light of the foregoing and upon the file in said cause,

IT IS ORDERED that plaintiff's motion for a preliminary and permanent injunction is denied;

AND FURTHER ORDERED that the three-judge court is dissolved.

The foregoing disposition is without prejudice to further consideration by the District Court of such other questions as may have been raised and as may be presented in further proceedings. The case is remitted to the Honorable Alexander Holtzoff, sitting as a single judge, for appropriate action.

/s/ JOHN A. DANAHER,
United States Circuit Judge.

/s/ ALEXANDER HOLTZOFF,
United States District Judge.

/s/ EDWARD M. CURRAN,
United States District Judge.

Dated: May 12, 1961.

(6232-3)

No. 931

In the Supreme Court of the United States

OCTOBER TERM, 1962

CARLOS MARCELLO, PETITIONER

v.

ROBERT F. KENNEDY, ATTORNEY GENERAL OF THE UNITED STATES AND RAYMOND F. FARRELL, COMMISSIONER OF THE IMMIGRATION AND NATURALIZATION SERVICE

ON PETITION FOR WRIT OF CERTIORARI TO THE UNITED STATES COURT OF APPEALS FOR THE DISTRICT OF COLUMBIA CIRCUIT

BRIEF FOR THE RESPONDENTS IN OPPOSITION

ARCHIBALD COX.
Solicitor General,
HERBERT J. MILLER, Jr.,
Assistant Attorney General,
Department of Justice,
Washington 25, D.C.

L. PAUL WININGS,
General Counsel,
CHARLES GORDON,
Deputy General Counsel,
Immigration and Naturalization Service.

INDEX

CITATIONS

In the Supreme Court of the United States

OCTOBER TERM, 1962

No. 931

CARLOS MARCELLO, PETITIONER

v.

ROBERT F. KENNEDY, ATTORNEY GENERAL OF THE UNITED STATES AND RAYMOND F. FARRELL, COMMISSIONER OF THE IMMIGRATION AND NATURALIZATION SERVICE

ON PETITION FOR WRIT OF CERTIORARI TO THE UNITED STATES COURT OF APPEALS FOR THE DISTRICT OF COLUMBIA CIRCUIT

BRIEF FOR THE RESPONDENTS IN OPPOSITION

OPINION BELOW

The opinion of the court of appeals (Pet. Br. 15–22) is reported at 312 F. 2d 874.

JURISDICTION

The judgment of the court of appeals was entered on December 20, 1962. The petition for a writ of certiorari was filed on March 14, 1963. The jurisdiction of this Court is invoked under 28 U.S.C. 1254(1).

(1)

QUESTION PRESENTED

Whether the court below properly ordered the dismissal of a suit for declaratory and injunctive relief challenging the legality of a prior deportation on the grounds (1) that the request for injunctive relief had become moot and (2) that the request for declaratory relief involved issues which could be litigated in and were solely of relevance to pending criminal and deportation proceedings in another circuit.

STATEMENT

A final order of deportation was entered against petitioner on June 1, 1953 for violation of the Marihuana Tax Act. The validity of that order was upheld by this Court in 1955. *Marcello* v. *Bonds,* 349 U.S. 302. Thereafter, the execution of the deportation order was delayed by petitioner's repeated appeals to the courts, including a suit in the Civil Court of Rome, Italy, for a judgment declaring him not to be a citizen of Italy and to enjoin the Italian Government from issuing a travel document to him. The chronology and nature of this course of litigation is set forth in H. Rep. 565, 87th Cong., 1st Sess., pp. 7–11.[1]

---

[1] The Committee report indicates that the assertedly dilatory and repetitious litigation by petitioner and other deportees was a major reason for the subsequent enactment by Congress of Sec. 5 of the Act of Sept. 26, 1961, 75 Stat. 650, 651, providing a single, expeditious remedy for the review of deportation orders. See also H. Rep. 1086, 87th Cong., 1st Sess., pp. 22–30. Another comprehensive recital of the prolonged maneuvers by petitioner to defeat the deportation order against him appears at J.A. 201–228.

In the administrative proceedings, it was concluded that petitioner was a citizen of Italy. That conclusion was based on petitioner's testimony that he was born to Italian parents in Tunis, North Africa, on February 6, 1910. J.A. 15.[2] However, on February 14, 1961, the Italian Government furnished to the United States Immigration and Naturalization Service (INS) a photostatic copy of a birth record indicating that petitioner had been born in Palo Blanco, Guatemala, on February 6, 1910. In furnishing this document, the Italian Government informed INS that it had been transmitted to the Italian Foreign Ministry in Rome by the Italian Consul in New Orleans, Louisiana. *Id.*[3]

The actual existence of such a document was thereafter confirmed by visual inspection in Guatemala. *Id.* The certified record of birth apparently had been given to the Italian Consul in New Orleans by petitioner or by a person acting under his direction; no civil record of birth in Tunisia had been located; and there were other discrepancies in the account of the alleged birth in Tunisia. INS therefore concluded that there was reasonable basis for believing that Guatemala was the true place of petitioner's birth and that deportation to Guatemala would be proper. J.A. 15–16. A representative of INS thereupon conferred with the Chief of the Immigration Service of Guatemala, acquainting him with the foregoing facts and asking whether the Government of

---

[2] References are to the Joint Appendix in the court below, which has been lodged with this Court.

[3] A copy of this birth certificate, with a translation, appears at J.A. 94–96–B.

Guatemala would issue a travel document for petitioner and accept him as a deportee from the United States. J.A. 16, 19. The Immigration Chief of Guatemala replied affirmatively and issued a travel document for petitioner on March 15, 1961. J.A. 16, 20, 92–93.

Upon receipt of the travel document, INS decided to deport petitioner to Guatemala. It was advised by its General Counsel that, contrary to petitioner's contentions, deportation was not inhibited by any judicial or administrative restraint or by any agreement.[4] J.A. 17. On April 4, 1961, petitioner was taken into custody under the order of deportation and he was deported that day to Guatemala. J.A. 21–24, 56.

The following day, this suit for a declaratory judgment and an injunction was commenced by petitioner in the United States District Court for the District of Columbia. J.A. 1, 4. Petitioner's complaint

---

[4] Petitioner now contends that the government had stipulated that he would not be deported without three days' notice. The document to which petitioner apparently refers was filed in the Supreme Court on October 10, 1955, and states in full:

"It is hereby stipulated by and between counsel for the respective parties herein, that the petitioner will be released upon administrative bail in the amount of $10,000, conditioned for his delivery into custody for deportation upon three days' notice, that such bond will be substituted for the judicial bond previously executed herein and that, in view of the foregoing, counsel herein consent to the vacating of the Order of Mr. Justice Black dated September 16, 1955." (J.A. 71.)

The provision for three days' notice was plainly a condition for forfeiture of the $10,000 bond and nothing else. Moreover, the administrative bail bond was cancelled on April 26, 1956, and the stipulation thereupon lapsed. Upon the expiration of six months from the final deportation order INS had lost its authority to require further administrative bail. *Shrode* v. *Rowoldt,* 213 F. 2d 810 (C.A. 8).

attacked the legality of his deportation to Guatemala, contending that respondents and their agents had made false representations to Guatemala, had denied him advance notice and the assistance of counsel, and had violated his constitutional rights. J.A. 4–6. Simultaneously, petitioner moved for a preliminary and permanent injunction to require respondents to return him to the United States and to restrain them from enforcing the deportation statute against him. J.A. 9.

A three-judge court found the statute constitutional and then remanded the remaining issues in the case to the district judge for further appropriate action. J.A. 26–27, 194 F. Supp. 748 (D.C.). Cross motions for summary judgment were made and, on May 24, 1961, Judge Alexander Holtzoff ordered that summary judgment be granted in favor of respondents and that the action be dismissed. J.A. 49–50. A motion for reconsideration was denied on June 5, 1961. J.A. 50. On June 9, 1961, petitioner moved to vacate the summary judgment, asserting that he had returned to the United States following his expulsion from Guatemala, had surrendered to INS on June 5, 1961, and had been served with an order to show cause and notice of hearing in deportation proceedings. J.A. 50–51.[5] It also appears that a

---

[5] Following the illegal reentry, a new deportation order was entered against petitioner, which became final December 20, 1961. This new order, predicated on Sec. 242(f) of the Immigration and Nationality Act, 8 U.S.C. 1252(f), merely reinstated the previous order of deportation, which had been upheld by this Court. Petitioner has not sought judicial review of the 1961 order. Since more than 6 months has elapsed, his only judicial review would be by habeas corpus. See Sec. 106, Immigration and Nationality Act, as amended, 8 U.S.C. 1105a.

criminal prosecution under 8 U.S.C. 1326, predicated on the unlawful reentry, is pending against petitioner. J.A. 82.[6] On June 20, 1961, the motion to vacate the summary judgment was denied. J.A. 57.

Petitioner appealed from the orders granting summary judgment, denying reconsideration, and denying the motion to vacate. J.A. 63. On December 20, 1962, the United States Court of Appeals for the District of Columbia found that the district court should have dismissed the complaint in the exercise of its informed discretion. It ruled that, since petitioner had returned to the United States, the cause had become in large part moot, and that, while some aspects of the complaint still presented a live controversy, those issues could more appropriately be settled in the pending criminal prosecution for unlawful reentry following deportation. The judgment and orders on appeal were vacated and the case was remanded to the district court with directions to dismiss the complaint. Circuit Judge Wilbur K. Miller dissented, declaring his belief that the district court had properly entertained the action and had correctly ruled against petitioner on the merits.

ARGUMENT

The decision of the court below, which grants petitioner the very disposition of this case which he re-

---

[6] In addition to the unlawful reentry charge under 8 U.S.C. 1326, petitioner has been charged with violating the conspiracy and perjury statutes, 18 U.S.C. 371 and 1621. These charges relate to the alleged procurement of a forged Guatemalan birth certificate (Crim. Nos. 28365 and 28366, United States District Court, Eastern District of Louisiana).

quested of the district court, involves no issue of broad, or continuing importance such as would justify review by this Court. The decision, indeed, does not substantially affect the rights of the particular petitioner now before the Court.

1. Petitioner's complaint requested a declaration that his deportation to Guatemala was unlawful and an injunction ordering that he be permitted to return to the United States. On petitioner's return to the United States, the request for injunctive relief plainly became moot. Petitioner's request for declaratory relief retained practical importance only to the extent that a determination that he had been illegally deported might affect a pending criminal prosecution in the Fifth Circuit for illegal reentry or pending deportation proceedings based upon illegal reentry after deportation.

The decision of the district court was that petitioner had been legally deported to Guatemala. The only available dispositions of the case in the court of appeals were to affirm, to vacate as petitioner had originally requested, or to reverse the summary judgment and remand for trial of the disputed issues of fact. The court of appeals concluded, entirely reasonably, that the district court's declaratory judgment should neither be affirmed—thus casting serious doubts upon the proper course of the pending prosecution and deportation proceedings— nor reversed for trial in the district court of an issue which had practical importance only as it related to pending proceedings in another circuit where, if the issue is held to be relevant, it can still be fully and fairly litigated.' The court of appeals therefore decided that the judgment of the district court, which was adverse to the petitioner, should be vacated as petitioner had requested.

This disposition by the court of appeals falls well within the traditionally broad scope of a federal court's equitable discretion in denying declaratory relief. *Great Lakes Dredge & Dock Co.* v. *Huffman,* 319 U.S. 293, 300; *Eccles* v. *Peoples Bank,* 333 U.S. 426, 431. The court here was influenced by the uncertainty its declaratory judgment would produce in other proceedings where the issues could more appropriately be tried. See *Rescue Army* v. *Municipal Court,* 331 U.S. 549; *Public Service Commission* v. *Wycoff Co., Inc.,* 344 U.S. 237, 243. It also realized that its decision in the declaratory judgment suit might not preclude petitioner from raising the same contentions in defending the criminal prosecution for unlawful reentry after deportation. In that event, its declaratory judgment would be only advisory and would not determine a case or controversy warranting the exercise of judicial power. See *Aetna Ins. Co.* v. *Haworth,* 300 U.S. 227. The discretionary refusal to grant declaratory relief in these circumstances was entirely proper. See 6 Moore, *Federal Practice* (2d ed.) 3032 *et seq.*

' In our view it is questionable whether petitioner can properly resist a prosecution for unlawful reentry by contending that his deportation was invalid, thus bypassing other processes for adjudicating his grievance as well as the established mechanism for the control of entries into the United States. If this issue is not relevant to the pending prosecution, it is all the more clear that the district court's declaratory judgment was properly vacated.

. The court, we emphasize, did not foreclose the presentation of any allowable challenges to the deportation, but concluded only that they should await disposition in a more appropriate forum in pending proceedings. The review petitioner can obtain in those proceedings is at least equivalent to that available in this declaratory judgment suit. The court below, far from deciding an important issue of federal practice, as petitioner contends, exercised an informed discretion in a situation which is unmistakably unique.

. 2. There may be some question as to the occasions on which it is proper for a three-judge district court, which has denied a plaintiff's constitutional claim for injunctive relief against the enforcement of a federal statute, to remit to a single district judge the decision of other issues or of claims for other than injunctive relief. See *Public Service Comm. of Missouri* v. *Brashear Freight Lines,* 312 U.S. 621, 625. But there is no need in the present case to undertake further consideration of this question, which appears to have arisen extremely infrequently in the federal courts. At the time petitioner initiated this suit, which was prior to his return to the United States, he could in no way be affected by any threatened application against him of the provisions of 8 U.S.C. 1253(a)(7) and therefore the relief available to petitioner could not include an injunction "restraining the enforcement, operation or execution" of that statute. Accordingly, a three-judge court was not required by 28 U.S.C. 2282. Subsequent to petitioner's reentry the government has neither threatened nor attempted to deport petitioner again to Guatemala. Therefore, no justiciable controversy as to the constitutionality of a proposed enforcement of the federal statute has existed at any time during this litigation.

It would, in any event, be inappropriate to undertake review of the necessity for a three-judge court in the present case. It is plain that, even if a three-judge court were impaneled, it would properly and at once dismiss the complaint for declaratory relief so that all substantive issues could be determined in another circuit in the course of the criminal or *habeas corpus* proceedings to which these issues are alone relevant, if they are, in fact, of practical importance at all.

CONCLUSION

For the reasons stated, it is respectfully submitted that the petition for certiorari should be denied.

ARCHIBALD COX,
Solicitor General.

HERBERT J. MILLER, JR.,
Assistant Attorney General.

L. PAUL WININGS,
General Counsel,

CHARLES GORDON,
Deputy General Counsel,
Immigration and Naturalization Service.

MAY 1963.

www.ingramcontent.com/pod-product-compliance
Ingram Content Group UK Ltd.
Pitfield, Milton Keynes, MK11 3LW, UK
UKHW051835020125
3930UKWH00046B/705